Professor Birdsong's

BEST!

207 Dumbest & Weird

Criminal Stories

Leonard Birdsong
Winghurst Publications

Professor Birdsong's - BEST! 207 Dumbest &
Weird Criminal Stories
by Leonard Birdsong

© 2015 Leonard Birdsong
ISBN: 978-0-9898452-5-0

Winghurst Publications
1969 S. Alafaya Trail / Suite 303
Orlando, FL 32828-8732
www.BirdsongsLaw.com
lbirdsong@barry.edu

Disclaimer:

The facts that are recounted in the stories in this volume are true and in the public domain, as best as Professor Birdsong can determine from his research of court documents, newspapers, and wire services. The author's commentaries on these stories are his own views and opinions and do not reflect the official policy or position of any Law school, Law firm or other organization with which the author may be affiliated. The opinions provided herein are not intended to malign or defame any religion, ethnic group, club, organization, company, individual or anyone or anything. The author further covenants and represents that the work contains no matter that will incite prejudice, amount to an invasion of privacy, be libelous, obscene or otherwise unlawful or which infringe upon any proprietary interest at common law, trademark, trade secret, patent or copyright. The author is the sole proprietor of the work and all parts thereof.

Permissions:

Cover graphics:
© Elsyl|Dreamstime.com
© Dung Tran Thi|Dreamstime.com
© Route55|Dreamstime.com

Book cover design: Rik Feeney / www.RickFeeney.com

TABLE OF CONTENTS

INTRODUCTION

Professor Leonard Birdsong received his B.A. degree from Howard University and received his law degree from the Harvard Law School. After a rewarding career as a lawyer and diplomat he now lives in Orlando, Florida where he teaches Criminal Law, Evidence, and Immigration Law. He has written many scholarly legal articles since joining the legal academy. His latest scholarly piece is entitled: *Reforming The Immigration Courts of the United States: Why Is There No Will To Make It An Article I Court?*

This publication is not one of those scholarly pieces!

This volume of *Professor Birdsong's Best* is a collection of his favorite funniest 207 stories culled from the ten humor books he has written since 2010. The Professor has had fun bringing you stories from his two series, *Dumbest Criminal Law Stories and Weird Criminal Law Stories*. He writes these books just for his fun and for your reading enjoyment. This volume should bring you many good laughs. Professor Birdsong knows that it is good to get a good laugh at least once every day. That is why several years ago he began to collect and edit from the wire services and news the type of weird and funny criminal law stories about dumb criminals that appear in this volume.

Professor Birdsong wishes to thank all of his past brilliant student research assistants for their editorial assistance in helping to make this volume possible. You may find other volumes of Professor Birdsong's Dumbest Criminal Law Stories and his series of Weird Criminal Law Stories at Amazon.com or by going to his website: LeonardBirdsong.com.

Enjoy!

CHAPTER ONE

Would you say it was an A cup or a B cup sized condom? A cross dressing man in New York City snatched a purse from a 74 year old woman, but left behind a strange clue -- a condom filled with water that he had been using as a fake breast. The suspect, clad in a short denim skirt and black tube top, fled the scene in a car with two other transvestites. Police are checking the condom for fingerprint and DNA evidence.

Yep, hard times all over. Police arrested a Charleston, WV, man who tried to rob a video store with an empty cheesecake box. Paul Parrish II, 43, of Charleston placed the box on the counter of the Movie Gallery with a note that said it contained a bomb. The clerk refused to give Parrish any money and Parrish ran out of the store. He was soon arrested and told police he needed money for gas and cigarettes.

This one sounds rather gay. A Fresno, California house burglar rubbed spices over the body of a sleeping man before using an 8 inch long sausage to slap the face of another snoozing resident. Antonio Vasquez fled but was caught in a nearby field after police found his wallet and ID in the victims' home. The sausage was eaten by a dog after Vasquez tossed it away.

A Pennsylvania bank robber was so furious when told that the tellers' tills were empty he threatened to file a complaint with management before fleeing. When the robber walked in, the tellers were on a shift change and waiting for their cash drawers to be filled. The indignant but hapless robber was caught 10 blocks away. "How dare they not have money for me to steal!"

Germany: *No! It was not armed robbery.* A man with no arms managed to steal a TV from a German store. He made off with the 24-inch set using clamps that had been attached to his body by an accomplice. "It's hard to believe that the sight of an armless man walking along with a TV clamped to his body did not get anyone's attention," a police officer remarked.

Germany: *Ouch! Ouch! Ouch!* A skinny dipper in Germany who had broken into a community pool after closing hours fled from police when they tried to arrest him. The man had a painful, prickly end to his night when he fled right into a hedge of nettles. Police had no problem finding him. "The cops just followed the sound of the screaming," said a police spokesman.

Findlay, OH: *That's funny....seems there may have been a violation of some "penal" code!* This really is a weird one. A woman called Findlay police one recent weekend to complain that her husband claimed that her daughter -- his stepdaughter -- had performed oral sex on him and was far better at it than her mom. Police made note of this crime against humanity but had to tell the woman it actually did not violate any part of the penal code.

Lynnwood, WA: *Is his manhood still intact? Inquiring minds would like to know!* A man accidentally shot himself in the testicles at a hardware store in Lynnwood. He was carrying his pistol in the waistband of his pants on a Sunday, and it accidentally went off, police said. It was reported the man's leg and foot were also injured.

Los Angeles, CA: *Sounds like Reuben do that voodoo that he do so well.....but it didn't work!* Lance Ito, the judge in the O.J. Simpson murder case of several years ago, recently sentenced a defendant to 12 years in another strange case. Rueben Hernandez was arrested after police pursued him on a high speed chase after he had bought six properties using fake Social Security information. At the home he was staying police found voodoo dolls dunked head first in cups of water with pins in their eyes. The dolls bore the names of the prosecutor and the detectives on the case.

Cleveland, OK: *Oh my...* Jail officials in Cleveland County dress inmates in hot pink shirts and yellow and white striped pants that some complain make them look more like clowns than prisoners. Jail officials say the new outfits make it easier to find escapees.

Wenatchee, WA: *Did they question him about how his rectum got so large?* Speaking of prisoners, here's another one. In Washington state a prison inmate smuggled in a cigarette lighter, rolling paper, a golf ball size bag of tobacco, another small bag of marijuana, a small smoking pipe, a bottle of tattoo ink and eight tattoo needles -- all in his rectum. The prison contraband was found after a worker found a plastic bag and duct tape in the toilet and questioned the man.

TEXAS: *The police could see he's nuts...* A man from the town of Kemah was arrested for riding his unicycle completely naked. He told police he liked the feeling of riding without any clothes on. Police said he was distracting other drivers.

ARIZONA: *Dunce!* A convicted killer begged for mercy at his sentencing in Phoenix. He told the judge, "I regret every moment of the day I beat a 90 year old man to death." His family was by his side and he said that he planned to change his life and leave prison as a better man. He then undermined his own case by turning around and flipping the finger to a television camera person. He received a 22 year sentence.

NEW MEXICO: *N-Sane... Police sans guns!* The town of Vaughn has a small police department of just two; neither of the two officers is allowed to carry a gun because of legal problems. The chief lost his gun over a child support issue and his deputy can't carry because of a domestic violence incident. The chief said not having a gun was no problem, "We have Tasers, batons, mace...stuff like that."

PENNSYLVANIA: *Security officers were lucky not to have gotten a bust in the mouth...* A suspected shoplifter fled topless from security officers. Aishana Clayton, 26, was nabbed at a Pathmark in suburban Philly. As Clayton was led to a security office she began to punch, bite and scratch at officers who grabbed her shirt, but she tore free and fled from the store to her auto. "Her breasts were swinging as she ran to the car," Upper Darby police superintendent Michael Chitwood said. She remains at large.

PENNSYLVANIA: *Flaming tampons. Why?* A couple in this state has been accused of trying to blow up a rival couple's car by stuffing flaming tampons down the gas tank. Patricia and Quentin Deshong didn't succeed in blowing up the 2006 Ford Fusion, but they did cause serious damage, according to police.

NEW YORK CITY: *Death by a street sweeping machine, how offal...* This horribly strange accident will probably lead to a successful wrongful death lawsuit. A slow-moving street sweeper truck struck and killed a man in Brooklyn near the Barclay Center, after a Brooklyn Nets basketball game. It appears that the 40-something-year-old victim was crossing Flatbush Avenue near Atlantic Avenue, at about 1 am and moved right into the path of the sanitation vehicle. At first the victim was able to get back to the curb upon hearing the driver honking his horn and yelling at him. It appears, further, that the sanitation driver believed the man was in the clear and continued on his path. As the machine was passing by, the confused victim suddenly fell into the street and was sucked up into the vehicle near the rear tire. The distraught driver remained at the scene until police arrived. He was not charged with any crime.

NEW YORK CITY: *Yes, yes, we know... It really was "junk" in their trunks!!* Two

Bronx neighbors were returning from the Dominican Republic when authorities caught the women by the seat of their pants – quite literally. Priscilla Pena and Michelle Blassingale had just arrived at JFK aboard a JetBlue airliner from Santo Domingo, when they were stopped by Customs and Border Protection officers. A drug sniffing dog had alerted officers when it neared Pena, the officers searched her luggage but found no drugs. When the officers initiated pat-down searches of the two women they discovered that each was wearing a "diaper" filled with cocaine rigged around their hindquarters. The women were charged with smuggling over six pounds of cocaine.

NEW YORK CITY: *CHOMP, CHOMP, CHEW...* A Manhattan appeals court refused to release accused "cannibal cop," Gilberto Valle, on bail after a prosecutor said the suspect described how his "mouth was watering," as he sized up a woman he planned to make his "next meal." The three judge panel at the U.S. Second Circuit Court of Appeals quickly and unanimously rejected Valle's bid to reverse previous rulings of three lower court judges. Valle, 28, will remain locked up in solitary confinement until his trial in March. During the Circuit argument, the prosecutor characterized the six year NYPD veteran as a danger to the community, describing how he schemed to kidnap, cook, and eat women, during internet chat sessions. Valle's public defender argued that these chats were no more than fantasy on a sexual fetish website. He insisted that Valle merely engaged in "role play" concerning kidnapping, killing, cooking, and eating women.

NEW YORK: *If the breasts do not fit you must acquit...* A new state rule requires all court officers to wear bulletproof vests. However, the breast constricting safety gear has no contoured room for breasts making it painful and irritating for women. According to female officers, the state Office of Court Administration has had so many complaints that the agency could be forced to temporarily curtail the bulletproof vest mandate. The problem appears to have begun after the agency opted to buy "unisex" or "unstructured" bulletproof vests instead of the more expensive ones fitted for breasts.

PENNSYLVANIA: *Bet there won't be too many more complaints brought to that phone store...* Talk about customer service! A worker at a Philly-area mobile phone store has been accused of stabbing a customer who had come in the store to complain about being double billed. The customer survived the attack.

NEW JERSEY: *Nincompoops like Campbell should not sire children...* It is reported that a "Hitler loving" dad who named his children after Nazi leaders has lost his request to visit one of his children in foster care. Heath Campbell's request to visit his child was denied by a judge after state officials removed his three children from the home based on evidence of violence in the home. Campbell, 40, came to court dressed in full

Nazi regalia and complained that he was being unfairly targeted because of his beliefs concerning the Nazi regime. Campbell and his estranged wife, Deborah, have four children: sons Adolph Hitler Campbell, 7 and Heinrich Hons Campbell, 2, and daughters JoyceLynn Aryan Nation Campbell, 6, and 5 year old Honzlynn Jeannie Campbell.

OHIO: *This fellow picked the wrong species to mess with.* An Ohio K-9 dog chased down and bit a suspect wanted on dog-fighting charges. As the man ran, the police dog grabbed him by the wrist and dragged him to the ground, where two-legged officers finished making the arrest. *ARF, ARF... Dog-fighting, indeed!*

OHIO: *If she cleaned the whole house she should've charged more!* A Cleveland area woman dubbed the "cleaning fairy" pleaded guilty to attempted burglary, admitting she broke into a Cleveland home in June, cleaned it, and left a bill for $75. The "fairy," Zoe Caleb, said she "wanted something to do."

OHIO: *We hope the bet was worth it.* Police officer Oliver Twist of Mentor was suspended from the Mentor police force after dipping his head into a bucket of urine to win a $450 bet. Police Chief Daniel Wright said it's not something he would expect one of his officers to do – even when off duty. After undergoing a medical evaluation, Twist was reinstated onto the force.

MICHIGAN: *Someone needs to treat himself to a vasectomy!*! A Michigan man has been sent to jail for failing to pay $500,000 in child support to 14 women with whom he has fathered 23 children. When this father appeared in court he could not even remember the names of all his children.

CALIFORNIA: *No sale!* A woman was arrested after she allegedly held up a bank during her test drive of a used car. The suspect told the seller riding with her that she just needed to pop in the bank and get some money. He didn't know how she got the cash until police surrounded them and arrested her.

CALIFORNIA: *Elders gone wild?* A 72 – year old woman and her 62-year old boyfriend were arrested for having sex in a car parked behind a BBQ restaurant in Sonora. The midday tryst shocked diners and police, who gave the aging, passionate pair a summons. *Sounds like they should have rented them a room, instead.*

ARIZONA: *If this program works, Tucson will become the new Dodge City!* A Tucson politician is raising money for a private program to hand out free shotguns to people in high crime neighborhoods. Sponsor Shaun McClusky plans to give people up to $400 to arm themselves and fight crime on their own. "Saying guns are responsible for killing people is like saying spoons are responsible for making people fat," he said.

TEXAS: *Talk about real low-lifes... Stealing a preacher's wallet in church.* A preacher's wallet was stolen by two thieves who went on a shopping spree around Fort Worth while he delivered a sermon on showing mercy to others. The pair ran up $2,000 in purchases on the Rev. Rob Hamby's credit cards. "What troubles me is that they would go to the church, not to help but to steal," Hamby said. "I am shocked and frustrated. "

LOUISIANA: *We wonder why she had to get naked?* A woman got into a taxi one afternoon in the small town of Covington and demanded that the driver take her to Michigan. We do not know why she wanted to go to Michigan or where she wanted to go in Michigan. Michigan was more than 1500 miles from Covington, Louisiana. The taxi driver refused to take her anywhere, they began to argue, and then she completely disrobed, leaving her clothes on the side of the road, and slid into the driver's seat and raced off in the taxi. The taxi driver, of course, called police who caught her after a brief chase. We strongly suspect she was impaired in some way.

UTAH: *We never learned why she was naked!* One bright, warm sunny, afternoon

Ms. Sylvia, 33, stole two cars and led police on a wild chase, all while she was naked. Sylvia was already naked when she came upon a man out on a lonely Utah road who had been hanging roadside signs advertising his business. Without any warning Sylvia stole the man's car and drove off. The businessman immediately called the police from his cell phone and gave his location and a description of his car. Two police cruisers rushed to the scene, spotted the car and began chasing Sylvia. Then, as officers chased her she got tricky and bailed out of the stolen car and began to run on foot. Both officers stopped their vehicles and gave chase to her on foot. Sylvia then speedily doubled back and jumped into one of the empty police cars and took off before crashing it. The entire incident took no more than fifteen minutes. When caught Sylvia was given a blanket and placed under arrest. *Again, Nope, we never learned why she was naked!*

FRANCE: *Booby Trap?* Paris is a lovely city without much serious street crime. However, in the spring of 2013, a crew of teenage girls in Paris was reported to be robbing men at ATM machines. Spring is always a beautiful time in Paris and there are an awful lot of ATM machines throughout Paris. How did the girls work it? It appears that the girls hung around downtown ATM machines that were near subway entrances and waited for young businessmen to withdraw cash, two of the girls would then distract the men by flashing their bare breasts, and the third girl would snatch their money before the men could pocket it. The girls would then run to the nearest subway entrance and make their getaway. The three girls who were arrested were found to have stolen about $1,000. Not a bad haul for high school girls.

FLORIDA: *Freelance stripping?* Clearwater Beach, Florida really does have some of the most beautiful, clear water of the entire Gulf Coast. It is a great little city with wonderful people. Not too long ago, a Clearwater woman was arrested after she walked into the Baby Dolls gentlemen's club in Clearwater, took off her clothes, got on stage and started dancing for tips. Some gentlemen's clubs in other states actually encourage this kind of behavior. However, this is not the case in Florida. The woman, Nadia Botkins, was not employed by the club. It was the real dancers who called the police on her. She was arrested. The lesson to be learned: *No freelance stripping in Clearwater Beach?*

CALIFORNIA: *No jiggle with their java?* Police in San Jose cited three women working in a local coffee house for public nudity for allegedly serving customers while topless at the Quyen Café. We learn that there had been an ongoing fight in San Jose between city officials and coffee houses in the Vietnamese neighborhood, where servers often worked in revealing clothes. In the past, other cities such as Fort Lauderdale, Florida found there were no regulations against women serving coffee topless, however, these businesses did not thrive and soon went out of business. Perhaps, coffee house patrons do not prefer jiggle with the java!

CANADA: *OH POOT!* Police in Ontario have announced the winner of their silliest excuse competition. Oh yes, police do have such competitions. Here is what we know about the winner of their latest silliest excuse competition. The winner was a woman stopped for speeding who explained that she accidently stepped on the accelerator when she adjusted her seating position to fart. *Yep, silliest and smelliest excuse, without a doubt.*

JAPAN: *They describe him as homeless, but "well-heeled."* An unemployed Tokyo man with no permanent address kept 450 pairs of women's high heels that he had stolen in a rented room. Soho Shoso, 28 told police "I've felt pleasure in stealing high heels. I was not interested in brand new products."

JAPAN: *Surely a pervy weirdo…* A 38-year-old Tokyo police officer, who reportedly admitted to friends that he wanted to be a high school girl, was fired recently for allegedly dressing up in a sailor girl outfit and exposing himself to a 16 year old teen. The report indicates that the officer had previously been arrested for exposing himself in public.

JAPAN: *Meow!* A man on a yearlong burglary spree stole nearly $180,000 in cash and valuables to feed his 120 cats a gourmet diet, according to police. Mamoru Demizu, 48, of Izumi city is suspected of breaking into houses 32 times to provide the $250-a-day cat feast.

CHINA: *Murder, by way of malicious gonad grabbing?* A woman has been accused of killing a man by squeezing his scrotum. The gonad attack came when the man complained to the woman about parking her motor scooter in front of his store. The argument got so heated that the woman grabbed the shopkeeper and yelled, "I'll squeeze it to death! You'll never have children again!" Her grip was so strong the man went into shock and died.

CHINA: *Sex slows*. Lin Chen, a 67-year-old woman who lives in Ningbo, who believed that police were not doing enough to stop speeding drivers on her street came up with a brilliant idea. She tied a blow up sex doll to a tree outside her house. This prompted drivers to slow down to gawk and wonder why. Police contend that since the doll went up, traffic accidents have gone down. Who knew?

Could we say the bond between this lady and her dog failed? A Tampa woman was arrested for using glue to close up her dog's Caesarian section. The dog had trouble giving birth, so she sliced the dog's stomach open. The mama dog died and the woman was charged with animal cruelty. We learn that the pups lived.

This was a funny police report. It read, in part: "Police arrested a man for bringing a pussy into a strip joint." Managers at the Emerald City gentlemen's club in the town of Murdock refused to allow Everett Lages, 47, and his pet kitten into the club. The intoxicated Lages became angry and telephoned 911. He was taken into custody for misuse of 911, trespassing and disorderly conduct. The kitten was put in the safe hands of animal control. *No pussies allowed in a strip joint – who knew?*

This is what happens when "inquiring minds would like to know." Florida police nabbed one of their own snooping on his ex-wife's boyfriend, a local TV news anchor and tennis star, Anna Kournikova. The Clearwater Police Department's Internal Affairs Bureau caught the police lieutenant accessing state motor vehicle records to obtain the addresses of 54 people not connected to any crimes. He is now facing demotion or termination.

Criminal Barbering? Veteran's Day weekend, 2010, the Orange County Sheriff's department became a national laughingstock when it was reported that sheriff deputies and members of the Florida Department of Business and Professional Regulation carried out a series of warrantless raids against local Orlando barbershops that made history for arresting 35 people on misdemeanor charges of "barbering without a license," after having spent several months investigating the matter. A records check revealed that in the last ten years only three people in the entire state of Florida went to jail on such charges. In the instant cases, many of the warrantless sweeps entailed officers swarming the barbershops that had children inside and putting the barbers in handcuffs and "perp walking" them to police vehicles. We learn that one felony arrest was made when one of the raids netted a barber with an unlicensed handgun. We learn further that all the barbershops were in the African American and Hispanic neighborhoods. Obviously, those neighborhoods are "hotbeds" of criminal barbering.

CHAPTER TWO

TURKEY: *No one knew because they were such good thieves!* Thieves stole an entire 82-foot, 44,000 pound steel bridge that went over a creek in a rural province. No one knows how they were able to dismantle the entire structure without anyone knowing, but they are believed to have taken it to sell for scrap.

TURKEY: A court in Istanbul formally arrested a Ukrainian man who allegedly tried to hijack a turkey bound flight to Sochi, Russia, as the winter Olympics were beginning. The Anadou News Agency reported that the man, AK, was ordered jailed following questioning by police. It was further reported that the man claimed he had a bomb and tried to divert the Pegasus Airlines flight, which originated in Kharkiv, Ukraine.

The pilot tricked him and instead landed in Istanbul where he was subdued by officers who had sneaked on board. Ukrainian officials maintain that AK tried to hijack the plane to press for release of anti-government protesters in his country.

ZAMBIA: *Sounds more like they're having wet dreams!* It has been reported that teachers in Zambia are threatening to quit over "invisible witches" sleeping with them at night. The report goes on to maintain that educators in Siavonga have packed their belongings and are ready to flee, claiming "wizards and witches" are forcing them to have sex. "The male teachers complained that they have been having sex with women they cannot see," said traditional leader Chief Sinadambwe, who is calling on the government for help.

ITALY: *Merry Dildo?* An outdoor Christmas tree in Milan had to be cleaned up after city officials removed dildos and other sex toys that had been placed on the tree as ornaments.

A Milanese woman who has launched an Italian sex toy e-commerce website defended the "Tree of Pleasure," which she said was intended to end taboos by making the items "normal everyday objects."

ITALY: *OINK!* It has been reported that a still-breathing Italian mob boss was fed to the pigs by members of a rival crime syndicate. Francesco Raccosta was beaten with iron bars by members of the N'drangheta crime family which controls much of the southern Italian region of Calabria. They then tossed him in the pig sty where he was eaten alive. The murder was allegedly carried out by mob boss Simone Pepe, 24, who admitted to the killing and three other murders. Raccosta had been missing for more than a year when authorities arrested Pepe and gained his confession. A police spokesman said the bloody feuds between the rival crime clans had been ongoing since the 1950's.

This is so weird...butt lifts performed in a motel room! The headline read: "She wasn't just a phony plastic surgeon; she was also a phony woman." A man was arrested in Palm Beach for allegedly giving people illegal butt enhancements without a license – and while posing as a woman. The victim's first hint that something might have been wrong should have come when the suspect preformed the bogus lifts in a motel room. *Butt lifts???*

Damned if she do and damned if she don't.... A Florida city manager who was fired for undergoing a sex change operation is in trouble at her new job. Why? It has been alleged that she is a homophobe. After being fired Susan Stanton became a hero to the gay and transgender communities, and found a job in the open minded town of Lake Worth. However, after she criticized a gay bar owner over a noise issue, activists called her anti-gay and demanded she be fired.

BOOM? A woman was arrested after she drew a picture of a bomb and wrote the word "Boom" on her friend's suitcase as a prank before the friend left for the Miami airport.

The friend tried to check the bag with the bomb picture on it. This caused a major airport alert. The friend was not arrested but we are uncertain whether she made her flight.

*Ridiculous – No bail for failing to pay $85...Oh yeah, she was 23 years overdue! My bad...*A Disney dream cruise ended in a bad dream for a Connecticut woman over a shoplifting arrest 22 years ago. Robin Hall, 41, who works for aerospace manufacturer Pratt & Whitney, was arrested as she left the ship in Florida when federal officials conducting routine security checks found the open warrant for her 1991 arrest for allegedly having failed to pay $85 in court costs. She was being held without bail.

The headline read: "If you are going to be a squatter, think big." Andre Barbosa, 23, moved into a vacant, five bedroom, $2.5 million home in Boca Raton, claiming the foreclosed residence under Florida's "deed of adverse possession' law. Bewildered police decided to leave Barbosa alone in the house and let the bank holding the mortgage fight it out with Barbosa in court. *If you are gonna squat – squat big Barbosa. Squat big!*

SWEDEN: *We wonder what her husband had done to her?* A woman admitted stabbing her husband to death with a fillet knife she had received as a Christmas present from her employer. She contends that the stabbing was in self-defense. Swedish police said that after the attack on her husband, Jeanette Javell, 42, wrote a bizarre note to her boss stating, "Thank you for the Christmas gift…By the way it worked!" *We suspect these words in the note may have provided evidence of a conspiracy between the woman and her employer. A conspiracy is defined as an agreement between two or more people to commit an act that is illegal and at least one of the conspirators undertakes an overt act in furtherance of the conspiracy.*

ITALY: *Too much T & A?* This one is about a lady who was too well endowed. Police report that a 31-year-old model was arrested by Italian authorities trying to smuggle more than five pounds of cocaine in fake breast and buttock implants. She had arrived at Rome's airport, and her plunging neckline caught the eye of security officers. This led to a search and subsequent arrest.

AUSTRALIA: *BUMCRACK?* Police are looking for "The Bumcrack Bandit." Authorities say the female felon held up a hotel bar and the only clue is a surveillance video of the woman making her getaway with her pants hung low which exposed her butt crack (or "bumcrack,"as they say in Australia). Police are now asking the public's help in identifying the behind behind the theft.

EGYPT: *Instant marriage on the rocks, or poetic justice?* A husband in Cairo watching a pornographic film was startled when he recognized the woman in the steamy sex scenes – it was his wife! When he confronted his wife of 16 years and the mother of their four children, at first she denied it was her in the film. However, she relented and finally told the husband that she had never loved him and that the man in the film was an old boyfriend she had before she got married.

UNITED KINGDOM: *Shhhhhhhhhhhhhh...!* Freedom of speech has its limits! A British woman lost her appeal against a court ordered ban of her deafeningly loud sex sessions, which led neighbors to call police -- thinking someone was being killed. Caroline Cartwright, 48, said it was a violation of her human rights, but a judge said it was actually just a "nuisance."

MONTANA: *What a zany jail sentence.* A Montana man is going to be spending the next five Christmases and New Year's Eves in jail – but he will be free the rest of the time. A judge gave Daniel Martz a 10 year suspended sentence for attacking a woman during the holidays, but ordered that he must be locked up from December 15 to January 1 for each of the next five years. The judge reportedly said that the holidays in jail will help keep

Martz out of trouble. *MERRY CHRISTMAS…..NOT!*

WYOMING: *ZAP*! When police responded to a domestic violence call at Brian Mattert's Cheyenne house he thought he had a surefire way to avoid being Tasered. Mattert covered himself in white latex paint and told police that if they Tasered him he would die. They Tasered him anyway – twice. Mattert survived and is now under arrest.

COLORADO: *How is this for irony?* An arson inspector was investigating several incidents in which automobiles had been set on fire along a street in Denver. As he was investigating, someone sneaked up and ignited his van, setting it on fire. The van suffered major burns on the left side. The inspector was said to be boiling mad over the turn of events.

OKLAHOMA: *Expensive Venison?* An Oklahoma state legislator shot a deer while out hunting. He then called the media and bragged about his hunting skills. However, there was a problem -- state Representative Terry Harrison did not have a hunting permit. He was fined $296.

MONTANA: *Dummy!* Federal agents were led straight to a man wanted for a fatal beating because he had his name tattooed on his head. That made it easy for the agents to find Sterling F. Wolfname — even though he tried to tell them he was somebody else.

NEBRASKA: *The headline read: Police believe they have flushed out the toilet paper bandit.* The thief who masked his face by winding toilet paper around his head held up a store in Lincoln in April, 2010. He fled with an undisclosed amount of money, but left a clue -- a prescription pill bottle. Police arrested the suspect in mid-May 2010. *They're stupid! That's why police catch them.*

OKLAHOMA: *Their worshipers are called "Pastafarians."* After the state authorized construction of a privately funded Ten

Commandments statue at the Oklahoma Capitol, officials were flooded with requests for new displays, including one from the Church of the Flying Spaghetti Monster. However, the Oklahoma Capitol Preservation Commission has banned handling requests until a court dispute over the commandments monument is settled.

MISSOURI: *Assault and mockery?* A Missouri woman who attempted to run down a man with her car was arrested and then used her one phone call from jail to call and taunt her alleged victim. It is reported that a police officer who overheard the telephone call described it as "pretty ugly." Witnesses at the scene of the crime reported that the woman appeared under the influence of drugs. *You think?*

OKLAHOMA: *The headline read: "The Burglar's crime really stank."* A burglar was arrested by police in Oklahoma City after he stopped to take a dump in the homeowner's bathroom and forgot to flush the toilet.

Detectives obtained a DNA sample from feces that was left on toilet paper and linked it to Caim Watson, 20.

MISSOURI: *Bet this idiot will never try to carjack anyone again.* This one is about a carjacking gone terribly wrong. A Kansas City thief jumped on a woman's car armed with a handgun and demanded that she give him the car. She did not give him the car! Instead, she drove, with the carjacker on the hood, at a high speed to the nearest police station where she crashed into the building. Yes, the "jacker" did receive minor, but not life threatening injuries.

MAINE: *Irony?* We learn that Police Officer, Aaron Yeo, of Groveland was relieved of his duties and fired from the force after police authorities planted spyware on his work computer and found him looking for women on MySpace and watching body building videos, cartoon shows and other TV shows. Among those TV shows it seems like his favorite was "The Biggest Loser."

CONNECTICUT: *He shouldn't have let the little head rule the big head...* The AP reports that a state marshal in Hartford had to apologize for paying $15 for a lap dance when he went to a New Haven strip joint to serve a city tax warrant. William Nolan broke down crying and apologized during his testimony before members of a state marshal committee investigating the matter.

MASSACHUSETTS: *Yep, he hit the trifecta of persecution....* The library in Belchertown kicked out a local artist whose legal name is Lord Jesus Christ. While the library says he was banned for bad behavior, Christ says he is being persecuted for who he is. "I'm black, I'm transsexual and my name is Lord Jesus Christ." He said.

NEW HAMPSHIRE: *I would probably have used my winnings to pay off a few bills...* What would you do if you won the lottery? Paula Cahill of New Hampshire was caught a few months after winning $100,000 in the New Hampshire lottery, spending her cash to fund a massive drug bender, according to a report. The 51 year old was arrested for trying to buy 100 OxyContin pills and was then awarded with a trip to the county jail.

MASSACHUSETTS: *Ironic, yes?* Sheila Burgess is Director of the Massachusetts Highway Safety Division. The Boston Globe found that Burgess has 34 entries on her driving record dating back to 1982, including seven accidents, four speeding violations and one for failure to wear a seat belt. She is now on leave after suffering a head injury following an August 24, 2012 car crash.

SWEDEN: *Be careful what you tweet for, you might get it...* A Swede sent a number of Twitter messages to his local police station complaining that there were frequent speeding drivers on his street and that law enforcement should crack down on such dangerous law breakers. The next day police on patrol pulled him over in a speed trap and wrote him a $358 summons for speeding and dangerous driving.

CANADA: *He who lives by the pills gets caught by the pills...* We learn that an accused robber in Halifax, Nova Scotia, derived too much pleasure from his ill-gotten loot. The knife wielding thief demanded prescription pills from a pharmacist, police report. He swallowed most of the pills before fleeing the pharmacy. Police report further that they found him a short distance from the pharmacy – passed out "cold."

CANADA: *...More lucrative than cattle rustling.* We hear that a thief has found a new criminal specialty. The so called "Tailgate Bandit" has been annoying Calgary pickup truck owners, stealing dozens of tailgates from their vehicles. Tailgate theft is soaring, because an experienced bandit can pop one off in less than 30 seconds and sell it for $4,500.

GERMANY: *We always heard that it was the man who wanted more...* A man in Berlin called police to complain that the woman he took home for a one night stand was demanding too much sex! We understand that he had to lock himself on his apartment balcony to avoid her loving advances. He called 911 and amused police officers showed up to save him from his predicament.

Winsted, CT:. *A Pup Tent Pervert? Yep, jail is where he belongs.* A rapist and high risk sex offender in Connecticut was arrested after he pitched a tent and lured children inside with candy and ice cream. Robert Logan, 34, a registered sex offender from Arkansas was charged with fourth degree sexual assault and breach of peace. Police say Logan offered candy, ice cream and money to several children one July weekend after pitching a tent at the edge of a parking lot behind an apartment building. A 7-year-old told her parents that Logan "pulled her bathing suit away from her bottom and looked at her bottom. The parents reported this to police. Logan denies anything inappropriate. Logan sits in jail with his bond set at $125,000.

Mobile, AL: *Eight children and nobody missed her! Sounds mighty suspicious...* Police believe a body found in a small time evangelist's home freezer is his wife and a mother of their eight children. Police arrested him on murder charges as he preached at a southern Alabama church. Anthony Hopkins, 37, was being held in jail awaiting a bond hearing. Police said no one reported 36 year old Arleta Hopkins missing, even though she had not been heard from in three years. The body was discovered in a freezer in a utility room during a police search of the home.

Indiana: *Maybe, Pochron needs to find a less dangerous line of work.* This one is about a new cop who got off on the wrong foot. Tim Pochron had been on the job for only 29 minutes during his first day on the police force when he wrecked his police car. In his defense, the other driver who crashed into him tested positive for drugs and was arrested.

Manhattan, NY: *Perhaps this is what is meant by sniffing out crime.* A cross-dressing bank robber donned a wig, makeup and women's clothing to throw police off the scent. Yet, he got caught because he could not disguise his large nose. Samuel Manoharan, 31, of North Bergen, New Jersey, was arrested as a suspect in five bank robberies in Manhattan and Brooklyn because police were able to clearly identify him from his profile taken by bank surveillance cameras – namely his nose, sources said. "He has very distinguishable features – a very large nose. His wig couldn't cover his nose," said a police source.

Ironic, no... The crime matched the costume. A Colonie, NY man dressed as a Breathalyzer unit for Halloween was arrested in Albany County for DWI. Theodore Piel, 24, actually refused to take the Breathalyzer exam, but still faces DWI charges. Arresting officers noted Piel's glassy eyes and a strong odor of alcohol, officials said.

Often the Lord protects little children, fools and teens high on mushrooms. It seemed everything was in slow-mo. A naked Virginia teenager high on psychedelic mushrooms was hit by a train but was unhurt because it was only going 9 miles per hour. Police found the youth lying comfortably under the train, and he ran off before deputies could get to him. They caught up with him in the woods several hours later.

Cherche La Femme, as the French would say. This one is not about robbery. This one is about a guy who had his beer and drank it, too. Dennis LeRoy Anderson was charged with DWI after crashing his motorized La-Z-Boy lounger into a parked car as he motored away from his local bar in Duluth. Anderson, 62, who had had nine beers before hopping into the contraption, claimed he was driving fine until a woman jumped in front of him, knocking him off course

CHAPTER THREE

Goodness, gracious, great balls of fire! Two boozed up practical jokers in the California town of San Luis Obispo decided to mess with their passed out drinking buddy by setting his crotch on fire. It was reported that the man suffered second degree burns to his testicles. Yes, a lot of alcohol was involved.

HIC! A man who walked into a convenience store in Waterloo, Iowa acted suspiciously and kept his hand in his pocket. The clerks, who had been robbed before, figured he must be a robber and threw a bag of money at him. He just looked at it and walked out. He was later arrested for public intoxication.

This is a record you would really not want to set. A Rhode Island driver was arrested by police and found to have a blood alcohol level of .491 – six times the legal limit – and the highest ever recorded in the state for someone not dead. Health officials say a .4 is considered "comatose" and a .5 is fatal. Police said "Our only assumption could be that the person has a serious alcohol problem."

...And probably not a moment too soon. A naked man was arrested in Kennewick, Washington for allegedly masturbating while chasing a garbage truck. John Foster says he chased the truck because he was upset that the driver had looked at him. Foster was charged with public drunkenness.

Tsk, tsk, too young to be a designated driver. In mid-August, 2011, a 35 year old Texas woman was arrested after she made her 12 year old daughter drive her to a bar outside Houston. Police spotted the obviously unlicensed girl driving erratically. She told police she had dropped off her mom who was afraid to drive drunk.

Chicago, IL, August, 2009: *Sounds horrible...a cross-dressing, chain wielding pickpocket in a dress...What next, Chicago?* A Somali born cabdriver, Abdinasir Kahin, wrestled with a cross-dressing, chain wielding suspected pickpocket in a dress and put him in a bear hug until police arrested him. The thief in the dress had already escaped from police once the same night after allegedly helping to beat a man bloody. While police struggled with the man's alleged partner in theft, Kahin saw the make-up wearing cross dresser return to grab a big white purse he had dropped before running away. That is when Kahin got out of his taxi and wrestled with and held the cross-dresser until an officer arrived to handcuff the thief.

Chicago, IL, August, 2009: *There should be a special place in hell for these four fools!* Prosecutors leveled additional charges Thursday against four Burr Oak Cemetery workers accused of illegally unearthing old burial plots to make room for new graves. Carolyn Towns, 49; Keith Nicks, 45; his brother Terrence Nicks, 39, and Maurice Dailey, 59, were originally charged with dismembering human bodies last month after authorities revealed the alleged grave selling scheme at the Cemetery where 1,200 bone fragments have since been found. Yet, now, in the formal indictment handed down by the Cook County Court, the four face two counts each of aggravated theft of $100,000 to $500,000, unlawful removal of gravestones, desecration of human remains, unlawful removal of deceased human beings from a burial ground and conspiracy to dismember human remains. The most serious felonies carry penalties of from six to 30 years in prison. Towns, who was the cemetery manager, allegedly masterminded the scheme, which prosecutors said began in 2003.

Chicago, IL, February 2009: *D'OH!!* This fellow wanted to get caught. A stupid bank robber in Chicago handed a teller a note – written on the back of his pay stub. The FBI was able to track him down easily when he left behind the note bearing his name and address. The dope faces 20 years in jail.

Chicago, IL, Christmas week 2009: *Someone should have called the "fashion police."* Three armed, masked men barged into a Chicago home a week after Christmas 2009, and forced 11 people to take off their pants. They then shot one of the victims in the leg. The robbers then fled with the pants and televisions. Police speculate that the pants were stolen in order to get the victims' wallets and to prevent them from chasing the robbers.

Chicago, IL, May 2010: *He must have been hungry and misses prison too.* A mugger took the breakfast from a disabled woman on the South Side of Chicago in early May. Charles Johnson, 35, grabbed a slice of pizza from the 21 year old victim afflicted with cerebral palsy. Johnson who has prior convictions for armed robbery, forgery and burglary also took the young woman's handbag. He was chased down by passersby and then arrested by police. He is being held on bail of $150,000, while awaiting trial.

CALIFORNIA: ....*Service minihorse? Did the stores fear horse droppings?* A paraplegic man is suing two stores in a California shopping mall after they refused to let him inside accompanied by his service animal. The animal happened to be a minihorse. The 29 inch pony pulled the man's wheelchair and he is seeking $4,000 from each of the businesses.

FLORIDA: *What the heck are they teaching students in Tampa?* A man in Tampa was recently arrested. Teacher William Chaney, 33, was arrested for allegedly head butting a student twice in class. Chaney who was charged with child abuse and battery was "horsing around" with a 13 year old student and head butted the boy twice, police say. The second hit came because the boy said the first blow did not hurt.

THAILAND: *Sniff....Sniff.... Phew!* Here's one for the books. Thai police recently arrested an underwear loving man who was holding 20,000 pairs of stolen women's underwear. The 48 year old man kept half of them in the trunk of his car, so that he could have access to them even on the go. "He smelled them all the time, even while driving," said a Bangkok police spokesperson.

FLORIDA: *Sounds like she was furnishing her own home...* Here's another one from Tampa. Sheriff's deputies in Tampa are searching for a woman caught on surveillance video walking out of a hotel room with a television, a bedspread, picture frames, an iron, an ironing board, rugs, a trash can and curtains. The room inside the Sabal Suites in Tampa was closed for renovation. We learn that the items, in total, were worth $700.

FLORIDA: *How large was the heart monitor? Was the gown open in back? Inquiring minds would like to know...* A jail inmate, being treated at a DeLand hospital, allegedly escaped from custody of authorities. Unfortunately, he made his getaway wearing a patient gown, in shackles and while attached to a heart monitor. Accused forger Michael Burke slipped out of a bathroom, but did not get far as he shambled down the street in his gown and shackles. Police soon caught him and put him under arrest for escape.

NEW YORK CITY: *That would have to be some outta sight sex for a million dollars – even with the haircut, massage and the Jacuzzi ride!* Accused Midtown "working girl" Janet Croom, allegedly asked an undercover police officer for $1 million in exchange for sex. It was a steep price, even considering police say that she offered to throw in a haircut, a massage and a "Jacuzzi ride." Of course, she was willing to discount, say police, as she haggled over prices with the undercover officer before her arrest, at Broadway and 52nd Street.

NEW YORK CITY: *I certainly wouldn't want to be the officer that had to fingerprint that stolen iPhone.* An ex-con was arrested for stealing an iPhone when it started to ring, while it was stashed up his butt inside a holding cell at a West Village police station. Trent Patterson, 47, had initially been arrested for an alleged burglary of a clothing boutique. While Patterson was in a holding cell, a 27-year-old man, whose iPhone had been stolen from him, used an app to track his device. The victim, who was at the station house to report the theft, called his phone – and heard the ringing coming from Patterson in a nearby cell. When an officer confronted Patterson he admitted he had hidden the phone up his butt. He was charged with criminal possession of stolen property.

NEW YORK CITY: *OMG, what a weird story...Just how desperate was Nancy for a baby?* A corrections officer at a federal prison was impregnated by and delivered the baby of a two-time cop killer in her care. She then insulted the victim's families by naming the child "Justus." Nancy Gonzalez, a federal corrections officer at the Metropolitan Detention Center in Brooklyn was criminally charged for her trysts with Ronnell Wilson. She delivered a healthy 7 pound 4 ounce boy. Gonzalez's sister maintains that "Justus" is a name from the Bible. It appears that Justus may have been the Disciple chosen by Jesus to replace Judas.

NEW YORK CITY: *Are tellers getting smarter or are bank robbers just becoming more stupid?* A would-be bank robber walked into a Manhattan bank hoping for a "sweet" payday – but left with nothing more than some hard candy, when a quick thinking teller would not cooperate. The robber handed the teller a note that read: "I have a bomb. Give me some money now." The teller was unfazed and defiantly stated, "I do not read notes." She then handed him a withdrawal slip on which he wrote, "I have a bomb." The teller then told him to swipe his bank card. She then turned to a fellow teller and told her in Spanish that she was being robbed. Upon hearing this, the crook said, "Ma'am I ain't got no time for this," groaned, and then grabbed a handful of lollipops from a bowl on the counter and ran out from the bank. He has not yet been found.

NEW JERSEY: *Hey, where's the beef?* Police are looking for a real life "Hamburglar" who stole $100,000 worth of patties from a warehouse in Linden. Their top clue is a video of a truck hooking up to the mobile shipping container at the port in Linden and driving off. The beef had come from Kansas and was destined for the Netherlands.

LONG ISLAND: *Crime doesn't pay, but it sure can bring in some big dough!* A couple was arrested for allegedly running a high end international prostitution ring that cleared more than a million dollars in the past two years, according to federal prosecutors. Vincent Lombardo, 43, and wife Melissa, 43, recently pleaded not guilty to money-laundering charges in Brooklyn federal court.

Evidence revealed that the duo's stable of pros raked in as much as $3,000 a day, of which the Lombardos took a 30% to 40 % cut.

MICHIGAN: *Is sex expected by the older men? If so, this sounds like prostitution...* This one comes from Detroit, a city going through bankruptcy. It has been reported that more than 200 of its public school teachers are moonlighting as "sugar babies" to make up for wage cuts or the loss of jobs. The report is derived from a website that matches up young women with "sugar daddies." The site reports that the average teacher can get up to $3,000 a month in return for providing companionship and pampering to an older man.

MICHIGAN*: Such a creepy story. Leave the dead alone!* Aiden Liam 49, pleaded guilty to sneaking into a Detroit graveyard and digging up the body of his late father, Claro Liam, with the intention of bringing him back to life. Authorities are not sure how Liam was going to bring his father back to life, but it is reported that he was caught after family members learned of his ghoulish plan.

OHIO: *Sounds like his neighbors should hide their inflatables!!* A man was arrested for allegedly having sex with an inflatable pool raft. A neighbor claimed his float was stolen by Miles Chase, who was allegedly seen getting it on with it. We learn further that in 2002, Mr. Chase was accused of having sex with a neighbor's inflatable Halloween pumpkin.

OHIO: *Are there no big girl tanning salons in Ohio?* A woman was banned from using tanning beds at one salon – because she was too fat. Molly Alexandra told a local TV station that she bought a $70 month long tanning package but she couldn't go into a bed because there was a 230 pound weight limit. To add insult to injury, the owner of Aloha Tanning refused to give her a refund.

TEXAS: *Que estupido?* Police in Dallas are under fire for giving tickets to drivers who do not speak English. The rogue language enforcers were slapping violators with $204 fines, even though there is no law saying drivers must speak English. Police Chief David Kunkle said he will cancel the fines.

TEXAS: *What an idiot!* Police in Austin said they arrested a former auto dealership worker who allegedly used a computer to disable more than 100 vehicles after he was fired. Austin police said Oliver Lopez, 25, who was fired from his position as a collector for Texas Auto Center in January, used his home computer on March 2nd to access the dealership's Web site and disable the engines and activate the horns of more than 100 vehicles sold by the business, an Austin newspaper reported. "He was the collector for Texas Auto Center, so he had the password and all the necessary requirements to get into the system and manipulate the vehicles," Sgt. Keith Bazzle said. The system is in place so the dealership can deactivate vehicles when customers fail to make payments, company officials said. They said further security measures are being implemented to prevent similar incidents in the future. Lopez was arrested Wednesday after police traced his computer's IP address. He was charged with felony breach of computer security and jailed in lieu of $3,000 bail.

NEW MEXICO: *El stupido y crudo, perhaps*....A clumsy burglar in Albuquerque was arrested after he tried to break into a college office and became tangled up in the venetian blinds as he crawled through a window. The accused burglar, Tommy Rivera, who was allegedly trying to steal computers became so entangled that he had to be helped out of the blinds bind by police before being taken off to jail.

TEXAS: *Bloody brilliant!* Microbreweries are pouring through a Texas sized loophole to make and serve beer. State law in Texas prohibits the brewing and sale of beer at the same location which has been seen as a slap in the face to these independent craft breweries. As a result many of these small businesses are skirting the law by brewing beer and selling glasses on the premises— which, just so happens to come with free beer.

MINNESOTA: *Ouch, Ouch, Hot, Hot, Can't see…stop, Ouch.…*A woman was arrested and charged with felony assault after she broke into a home and began blasting a man and woman – with a water gun. However, this was not really innocent play. The suspect had filled the water gun with water infused with red hot jalapeno peppers and squirted it into the faces of the victims. Although the report does not reveal all the facts, we are certain that the man involved was the husband of the woman with the water gun and that she had followed him to the house of his mistress. She may have to go to jail for this type of conduct, but we bet that "Ms. Watergun" is satisfied that she did what she had to do to try to get her husband back .

OHIO: *Her lover was probably inside the joint.* In the late summer days of two years ago a woman in the town of Hamilton was arrested for trying to sneak into the local jail. Deputies spotted her climbing over a barbed wire fence and into the rear yard of the lockup. When they ordered her to leave she asked them to arrest her. The deputies were pleased to oblige. They arrested her. Yet, deputies never seemed to care why she would try to sneak into a jail, over barbered wire, if it wasn't but for the fact that her significant other was on the inside.

MISSOURI: *BATTER UP!* A woman was arrested after she attacked her 21-year- old son's heroin dealer with a baseball bat. Violet London, who is 4 foot 10 and weighs 112 pounds, allegedly struck the dealer on both his arms after confronting him at his home. Despite her brave stand against drugs, she still faces assault charges. *However, this may be one way citizens can stem the tide of illegal drug use – by using the old fashioned baseball bat! BATTER UP!*

ILLINOIS: *Are our children safe anywhere anymore?* A four-year-old Chicago girl was listed as in good condition after she was wounded in the ankle while jumping on a bed where a handgun had been stashed under the mattress. An adult, Jarquise Upton, was charged with one felony count of unlawful use of a weapon. We have not learned her relationship to the child. What a freaky accident. Could the gun have gone off under the mattress and shot up through it to hit the child in the ankle. Inquiring minds would like to know.

AUSTRALIA: A burglar in Brisbane got much more than he bargained for when he was confronted by the 83-year-old homeowner, Edwin Dowdy and his wife. The two of them are trained in the Japanese martial art of Aikido. Dowdy contends the muscular burglar ran into the senior citizen's knife, leaving the fleeing burglar with a serious stomach wound. *So Aikido has something to do with knife fighting?*

AUSTRALIA: *OUCH!* What kind of sex was he planning on having? A man ended up in the hospital emergency room where he surprised doctors when an X-ray found that he had stuck a fork into his penis. The man had hoped the utensil would serve as a sexual aid. However, since this did not work out doctors removed the fork with lubricant and forceps. *OUCH! OUCH!*

SRI LANKA: It's hard to make a call when you butt dial! Have you ever heard of "butt-dialing?" Read this: A 58-year –old convict had his forbidden cell phone between his rear end cheeks when a guard came by his cell. And then… the phone rang. The guard confiscated the cell phone. We hope he used latex gloves to make the extraction.

MALAYSIA: *MOOOO...* Cattle rustlers don't get away! Thieves in Malaysia stuffed three full-sized cows into a tiny Proton Wira automobile, which is about the size of a Toyota Corolla. They had taken out the back seats for more room, but they didn't get far, as the animals weighed them down. Police eventually caught up with them and arrested them.

Hoodoo Voodoo! Were there zombies and the walking dead in the ring? Central Florida authorities recently announced the arrest of members of a meth ring that actually employed a voodoo priest. The voodoo priest served as a "spiritual adviser" to the ring's reputed leader "El Don" Florence. The takedown of the ring was dubbed operation Hoodoo Voodoo.

It certainly was some sort of weird homicide! Here's a weird and tragic story from DeLand, Florida. Marlon Brown, 38, was pulled over by police for not wearing his seatbelt. Dash-cam video from the police car showed that Brown got out his car and began to run. The police officer gave chase in his police cruiser and ran over and killed Brown. The manner of death was ruled an accident, however, the Florida Department of Law Enforcement Medical Examiners Commission has called the autopsy report into question. Although a grand jury did not indict Officer James Harris of any wrongdoing, he was fired and settlement was reached with the Brown family who received $500,000 from the city of DeLand. Brown's wife, Krystal contends that officer Harris should be charged with vehicular homicide.

Just how many bras can one woman wear at a time? A dragnet conducted by the Seminole County Sheriff's office just before Christmas 2013 resulted in 48 arrests, including a woman charged with stealing $1,700 worth of bras from a shopping mall. A part of the dragnet was comprised of plain-clothes deputy detectives who worked undercover inside a number of different stores.

*So humane....*A bandit carjacked a woman in a dangerous crime-ridden section of Orlando, but he didn't want to leave her defenseless in that part of town. So, he handed her a box cutter to defend herself from other possible criminals. He then said, "take care of yourself" and drove away in her Honda vehicle.

Assault with a dangerous weapon – rocky road. A Port St. Lucie woman spotted her cheating husband at a Walgreens drug store with his side girlfriend, so she attacked him with a tub of ice cream she had just purchased. We hear that the cheating husband was bruised and hurt while his wife was arrested on an assault charge. The ice cream was rocky road.

The headline read: "His plans fell through." Police responded to a silent alarm at a CVS pharmacy in Melbourne and found a maintenance hatch open. Moments later, a ski mask wearing man fell out of the hatch right in front of the police. An arrest was immediately made.

CHAPTER FOUR

CALIFORNIA: *The headline read: "She was on the bluff in the buff."* The story comes out of San Diego which is reputed to have some lovely beaches. This particular story was about a situation on a lovely sunny summer day in which San Diego police had to rescue a naked woman who was stuck on a 450 foot cliff above Black's Beach, a noted spot for nude sunbathing. Police got her down safely, gave her clothes – and a citation for disrobing in public. *Despite all that, we understand her tan looked fabulous! Wonder how she got up there?*

COLORADO: *On edge is one thing, getting naked is another!* The Denver International Airport is one of the busiest in the country. Lots and lots of people pass through there every day. A year or so ago a woman at the

Denver International Airport was told to extinguish her cigarette – inside the airport is a no smoking zone. Upon hearing the request she freaked out and took off all her clothes, according to a police report. The woman told police she was on edge and had not slept the night before. She was taken to a local hospital. No charges were lodged. *We hope that she doesn't always conduct herself this way when she is on edge.*

GERMANY: *Mistaken identity?* Female partygoers, at least twenty of them, at a bash in a Simmern apartment building erupted in cheers when men dressed as cops showed up at their door. Problem was they were real cops, acting on a neighbor's noise complaint and not the male strippers thought to be coming to the 30th birthday party. Germans who live in apartment buildings seem to hate noise – particularly at night. It is against the law throughout much of Germany to flush your toilet between midnight and 6 am if you live in an apartment building. "It was a bit funny for all sides," said a spokesperson for the Simmern police.

ILLINOIS: *They both sound a little too old for this type of stunt!* Police arrested two women for flashing their breasts at male golfers at the Woodlands Golf Course in the city of Alton. Emily Ella, 40, and Kaylee Cook, 41, did not have any clubs with them when police arrested them for showing off their bare tops. Why would women this age engage in such conduct? *Does the phrase: "It pays to advertise," come to mind. Indeed!*

ILLINOIS: *CHOMP…. It's only news when…* A woman was arrested for being drunk and disorderly and for biting her bulldog in the town of Lake in the Hills. The dog bit her back, but police decided that it was self-defense. "The dog was not charged," said Police Sgt. Mark Smith. The woman was charged! *It's pretty sick to bite your own dog, lady.*

OHIO: Last summer, an Akron woman was spotted panhandling in her bikini on the streets of the town holding a sign reading, "I'm not homeless. I need boobs." Hailey Bailey, 37, says she's begging for enough money to finance breast augmentation surgery (implants) to enhance both her chest and her self-esteem. *Although she may not have much self-esteem, seems she has lots of Chutzpa!*

TEXAS: *Poetic justice?* One windy, but pretty spring Saturday morning a Bowie County lady was working in her back yard. She became frightened when she saw a snake in the backyard, thinking that it might have been poisonous, she had her son set it afire. What a bad idea! The snake fled in agony into a brush pile – which ignited her lawn and then, fanned by the wind, grew into a full blown brush fire that burned her own house down.

TEXAS: *SCHMUCK!* A woman working at a Laredo liquor store took off her shoe and bashed an armed robber with her 7 inch stiletto heel. When other employees piled on him with their own makeshift weapons, the bandit ran for his life. He was soon caught and arrested by police.

TEXAS: *The headline read: "What a Dumb-Bass."* A fisherman is in trouble after his bass catch exceeded the limit by 35 fish, and he bragged about it on his blog. Muster Hoffman even allegedly posted photos of himself and his catch. This prompted 600 angry web responses as well as phone calls to gaming officials. Hoffman now faces $17,500 in fines.

ARIZONA: *Who knew?* The Arizona Supreme Court has ruled that creating a tattoo is a form of protected speech. The Phoenix suburb of Mesa had denied Ryan and Laetitia Coleman a business permit for a tattoo parlor, prompting them to sue, claiming that their free speech rights were being violated. A lower court dismissed the suit, but the state's Supreme Court reinstated it. They ruled: "Recognizing that tattooing involves constitutionally protected speech, we hold that the Superior Court erred by dismissing the complaint as a matter of law."

ARIZONA: *We had never heard of the charge of "giving a false impression of a terrorist act." It sounds silly…* A Phoenix man allegedly dressed his 16 year old nephew in a sheet and had him carry a fake grenade launcher in the streets, all to test police response time. Mitchell Turnblat, 49, was charged with giving a false impression of a terrorist act, endangerment, contributing to the delinquency of a minor and misconduct involving a simulated explosive. We learn it took police 15 minutes for police to respond.

ARIZONA: *This was not like Native Americans using psychotropic drugs to get closer to God.* A minister was recently arrested for allegedly selling parishioners heroin, meth and prescription drugs. However, Michael Benjamin, pastor of Faith Mountain Christian Church, maintains that he was only slinging the drugs to "bring them closer to God," according to the Maricopa County Sheriff Joe Arpaio.

NEW MEXICO: *Yes, Carlos, life is tough on the streets.* Convict Carlos Garcia spent five months hacking away at the bars of his cell window with a razor blade taped to a Popsicle stick until he finally cut through and escaped. But as soon as he got out he changed his mind and climbed back inside. He is now serving the remainder of his life sentence in solitary confinement.

MISSOURI: *The prospective renter was probably former chemistry teacher Walter White from "Breaking Bad," ha, ha, ha...* A tour of an apartment by a prospective renter in Springfield revealed the place had a kitchen, two full baths, and an unexpected luxury – a working meth lab. It appears to police that the drug den had been set up by squatters who were into methamphetamine production.

NEBRASKA: *...And also because she hasn't had any kind sex in twenty years!* Arlene Hald, 86, of Bellevue, recently received a $1,000 credit card bill for phone sex supposedly run up by her husband. Arlene is not mad at her husband — because he has been dead for twenty years and the couple never had a credit card! The billing company has agreed to remove the charges, believing Hald is a victim of identity theft.

OKLAHOMA: *What kind of grandma visits a junk yard with a six and seven year old, anyhow??*

Six and 7-year-old brothers in the town of Oktaha set off a police search when they went missing while visiting a junkyard with their grandmother. At the end of the three hour hunt, the pair was found in an empty house. They had ransacked the house, eaten a bunch of food they found there and painted their faces.

MISSOURI: *The headline read, "Who needs a job when all you need are paychecks?"* We learn that Violet Cathey, 30, of Springfield was arrested for allegedly forging payroll checks and cashing them at Walmarts in Arkansas, Illinois, Iowa, Kansas, Oklahoma and Missouri. The 515 forged checks totaled $116,295.99, Walmart reports. Cathey is unemployed. *Sounds like she paid herself a pretty good annual salary...*

MISSOURI: *This victim was a lucky hardhead!* A St. Louis man was shot in the head, but drove himself to the hospital, despite his wounds. The victim had been chasing the shooter in a car when they both got out of their vehicles in an alley and shots were fired. The victim is expected to live.

MASSACHUSETTS: *Reynolds was such an idiot – why not just take the key out of the ignition in order to stop the truck?* This guy received a summons after being struck by his own truck. Brian Reynolds, 40, was cruising in his 1987 Chevy when the brakes failed. He then tried to stop the truck by opening the door and dragging his foot on the ground. He then tried to turn up a hill but fell out and the truck drove over his left leg. Police gave him a $35 ticket for operating with defective equipment.

NEW HAMPSHIRE: *Will Bonnie and Clyde's descendants benefit from any of this?* The infamous bank robbers Bonnie and Clyde made only a few thousand dollars in their string of 1930's heists, but the guns they used fetched a whole lot more at a recent auction. Bonnie Parker's Colt .38 sold for $264,000 and Clyde Barrow's 1911 Army Colt .45 went for $240,000.

MASSACHUSETTS: *He sounds like a real wuss...* A Boston bank robber, Dmitri Long, 34, has been dubbed the "U30 Bandit" because he can rob a bank and be gone in under 30 seconds. He was caught after his latest heist and pled guilty. While awaiting sentencing he wrote to the Judge: "I would like to go home to my mom while she is still alive and still have time to start a family with my girlfriend before her biological clock runs out." Unfortunately, he is looking at a 20 year stretch.

MASSACHUSETTS: *A rolling dope possessed coke ….in his wheelchair!* An arrest was made at Boston's Logan airport of a man who tried to sneak cocaine into the States, hidden in the wheels of his wheelchair. Emmanuelli Rojas-Moraza, of Carolina, Puerto Rico, was found in possession of 200 grams of cocaine. Rojas-Moraza had a cast on his leg, but X-rays later showed his injury to be phony.

MAINE: *Yep, sometimes the police get it wrong. We smell, yet, another lawsuit in the making...* It has been reported that authorities in the town of Belmont attempting to arrest a probation violator, instead found themselves in a dangerous standoff with the head of the local militia. Mack Page, 63, was sleeping, when state troopers trained floodlights on his house and ordered him to come out with his hands up. "I challenged them – who the hell are you? Am I going to get Tazed? Am I going to get shot by somebody," Page recounted. The police were embarrassed when they realized they had the wrong address.

VERMONT: *Ironic, no?* One would think it unwise to drive drunk on the front lawn of the founder of Alcoholics Anonymous' house, no? It has been reported that a man was arrested for DUI after he allegedly drove onto the property of the historic home of AA co-founder Bill Wilson in the town of Dorset. The house still hosts AA meetings, which suspect Donald Blood may consider attending.

SWEDEN: *Did he ask both women and men to have sex with them?* We learn that a Swedish train passenger was sentenced to prison for getting high and taking off his clothes. The unidentified man was travelling from Gothenburg to Orebro when he got high on pot, took off his clothes and walked through the train asking other passengers to have sex with him.

GREECE: *Father Fraudster...* Greek police have reported that a childless former police officer invented 19 bogus children in order to claim benefits for all of them. He has been arrested. Officials contend that the 54 year old divorced man quit his $1,300 a month job in 2001 and had been living on the benefits.

GREECE: *Maybe the holy man had staked a claim on everything under the altar!* A Greek priest was arrested after he was caught digging for treasure under the altar of his own church. Neighbors alerted police of the priest's activities after they heard him drilling at night at the Church of the Prophet Elijah in the town of Eyska. The Priest's treasure hunt has been one of many reported lately in Greece since the country has been hit with huge economic woes, because of its debt problems.

EGYPT: *"Brainy" smugglers? They could have used Igor's help...* Egyptian customs officers confiscated 420 pounds of frozen cow brains that three Sudanese travelers were trying to sneak into the country. The brains, considered a tasty menu item in restaurants, could have netted the men $1,500, but were confiscated because authorities could not be certain that the brains had been properly preserved.

SYRIA: *Yes, this is certainly something the Assad regime would believe...* We hear that one of the world's top paid soccer stars has been drawn into the Syrian government's propaganda war. Lionel Messi, star for the team in Barcelona, Spain, has been accused by a TV station aligned with Syria's Assad regime of signaling smuggling routes to rebels in the way he passed the soccer ball on the field.

INDONESIA: *You think!!* Authorities there discovered 1,495 pig nosed turtles in two pieces of baggage heading out of the country.

The turtles, considered an endangered species, can grow as heavy as 44 pounds and are a favorite of smugglers. Authorities surmise that the turtles were being transported for resale.

MEXICO: *Ninny – this is no way to use a skateboard!* A would be bank robber rode up to a bank in Mexico City on a skateboard and announced a robbery. He may have made a strange getaway on his skateboard, but the teller set off a silent alarm and the robber waited while she counted out the money. Police then showed up and arrested the man.

GERMANY: *Yeah, diplomatic immunity does that to people...* Police in Germany were shocked when they caught the North Korean ambassador fishing illegally in a stream. When he was told to pull his pole out of the water he brazenly declared he had diplomatic immunity and kept his line in the water. After ambassador Ri Si Hong arrogantly waved authorities away, one police officer told reporters, "My colleagues are extremely frustrated."

SWEDEN: *Betcha they were faking it...* These folks certainly were not trying to keep their romance secret. A Swedish couple made so much noise in bed that their landlord tried to evict them. "Their screams of passion were so loud, I could hear them three floors away," said one building resident. "I don't think they were playing cards."

SCOTLAND: *Sounds like the words to that old song: Hold tight, hold tight, hold tight, I want some sea food mama...* This 22 year old woman in Scotland really loved her handbag. She held on so tightly when a man in a car tried to snatch away her Louis Vuitton that she was dragged down the street alongside the moving vehicle until he finally let go. The woman was hospitalized with cuts and bruises, but still has her Vuitton bag.

SWITZERLAND: *Shameful!* This one is about a driver who didn't do his bit for the environment. A Swiss driver accidentally hit the gas and plunged 30 feet into a giant recycling bin. The man was only slightly hurt, but was given a $75 fine for mixing metals and plastics.

RUSSIA: *She sounds like a "black widow." Men beware!* A 45-year old Siberian woman, who cannot stop killing her mates, was convicted of fatally stabbing her third lover and will now spend the next 12 years behind bars, according to authorities. Irina Rybalko, previously convicted of killing her husband in 1992 and a boyfriend in 1997, was sent to a prison colony, a Novosibrisk legal department spokesman said.

AUSTRALIA: *Weird stuff... a bra, ice cream and tuna! Ice cream and tuna do not mix well.* An Australian woman woke up to find an intruder standing over her bed, with her bra on his head and a tub of ice cream and a can of tuna tucked under his arm. The 61 year old woman then gave chase, hauling her catheter bag with her into the street, where the man was soon arrested.

MALAYSIA: *It's all about the "Benjamins!"* Malaysian police arrested a Lebanese man with $66 million in counterfeit US currency after he left a $500 bill as a tip for hotel staff. Since the largest US note in circulation is a $100, staffers called police who found him in possession of phony $1 million, $100,000 and $500 bills.

SWEDEN: *CROOK!* A Swedish man who claimed to be confined to a wheelchair was nabbed for swindling the government disability system after police found a photo of him dancing with a costumed rabbit mascot at an amusement park. His relatives were also charged because the swindler claimed they were helping care for him.

CHAPTER FIVE

Wow – just imagine how expensive a settlement it might have been if the bus driver had been eating caviar? A Jamaican beef patty cost a Florida county a pretty penny. A bus driver chowing down on the patty lost control of the bus, slammed down on the brakes and sent a dozen passengers sprawling to the floor. One of the passengers who had been seriously injured settled with Broward County for $100,000.

*What a loser...*A Tamarac, Florida man on a mission to steal toys from all 50 states was finally arrested after more than a decade of stealthy shoplifting that he used to pay for his vacations — including a trip to Hawaii. Ignatius Polara, 46, would allegedly steal from toy shops and then sell the stolen goods on eBay.

If one wishes to bribe their way out of trouble it is best to have a lot of money. We learn that a drunken bicyclist in Boynton Beach, Florida found that out the hard way after he was arrested for pedaling while intoxicated and he tried to bribe the arresting officers. He first contended he was a "professional MMA cage fighter," and then told the police, "fifty cents to let me go." The cops just laughed. When in the heck did it become illegal to pedal a bike when drunk? *This is not driving while impaired under the statute!*

Big mouth kids need to be shut up, but it was only a misdemeanor conviction. A Florida man was arrested after police pulled him over and his 7-year-old told the officers that the women in the back seat of the car were prostitutes. "Those are my daddy's hos'," the boy reportedly said. The father, Robert Burton was convicted of being a pimp.

Jesus! What next? A woman running for mayor of North Miami this last election season put up posters declaring she "is endorsed by Jesus Christ." Candidate Anna Pierre even had a picture of the Son of God on the ad. The "endorsement" didn't work with voters – she finished at the bottom in a field of seven candidates. *Jesus! What next?*

MEXICO: *A few more prostitutes and they can hold their first "ho down."* A group in Mexico has convinced the government to create the first retirement home for elderly street walkers. The home in Tepito, called Casa Xochiquetzal, can house up to 45 retired prostitutes, and now has 23.

"V" for Vendetta or victim? An off duty North Miami Beach police officer was arrested at an Obamacare protest rally in Plantation for refusing to take off a "Guy Fawkes" mask. Ericson Harrell, 39, was wearing a cape and the mask at the rally that has been popularized by the film "V for Vendetta," and often worn by Occupy Wall Street protestors. He allegedly refused to identify himself or show his face when officers asked him to. We understand that he

is now on leave from the North Miami Police department. He probably now thinks "V" is for "victim" of Obamacare.

Look for the suspect under the sea. Osceola County, Florida Sheriff's deputies are looking for a thief who was dressed like SpongeBob SquarePants as he robbed a 7-Eleven in the Orlando area. The police report advises that the suspect did not completely buy into the role because he only wore the SpongeBob mask. We learn there were no "SquarePants" worn.

OK! We get it...support her...bras for support. Yuk, Yuk. A Florida man loves his incarcerated girlfriend so much he shoplifted two bras for her as a gift, police report. Now Johnnie B, 29, is behind bars as his girlfriend prepares to get out of jail in a few days. After Mr. B was nabbed at WalMart he allegedly told police, "She has done so much for me... I felt I had to support her."

Wow! What a sentence. Timothy Anderson, 51, had been arrested in 2008 on child sex charges by Palm Bay, Florida police. In September, 2010, a jury convicted him of the sexual battery charges. Judge Dan Vaughn then sentenced him to 999 years, 99 months, and 98 days in prison. Authorities arrested Anderson after an investigation revealed that he had abused a girl from 1988 to 1991 on a near daily basis, beginning when she was six years old and in his care.

RUSSIA: *It was a Pussy Riot!* The Russian Supreme Court ordered a review of the case of two women from the band Pussy Riot, holding lower courts had failed to provide full evidence of their guilt and overlooking mitigating factors in sentencing them to two years in prison. The ruling may have meant shorter sentences for Nadezhda Tolokon-Nikova and Maria Alyokhina. Subsequently, during Christmas week, 2013 Vladimir Putin granted them amnesty and had them released from prison.

RUSSIA: *...And that is why one should always read the fine print!* A clever Russian tired of credit card offers turned the tables on that country's online bank by drawing up his own credit card contract and slipping it past bank officials. Dmitry Agarkov, 42, scanned the bank's contract and doctored the fine print to give him unlimited credit, a "0" percent interest with no fees or penalties ever – and the bank signed off on the deal. The bank sued Agarkov for $1,363 in late charges, but a judge ruled in his favor that the bank had signed and agreed to a valid contract.

POLAND: *It was not alive!* It has been reported that a disturbed Warsaw woman has been taken into custody for allegedly trying to create a Frankencat. Police raided her home and found live cats and dogs and the corpses of hundreds of pets, many of which had been cut up and crudely recombined. The home was filled with stench. The woman told police she was trying to make an 'undead" feline.

POLAND: *He sounds like a real boob!* A man has sued his ex-wife for a refund, noting that he had spent $8,000 on her breast implants while they were married. Lukasz Molovik's lawyer said his client suffered "loss of use" of the 32 DD implants. Molovik didn't need legalese to explain his action. "To be frank about it," he said, "I didn't spend all that money so some other man can ogle her breasts instead of me."

POLAND: *YOOOWWCCCCCCHHHH!* A man went under the knife for three hours to remove a screwdriver that had pierced his forehead. The 25-year-old man apparently lost consciousness after a fall. When he awoke he wasn't sure what had happened, so he went to his car, looked in the mirror and saw the screwdriver impaled just over his right eye. He had a cigarette, and then called a neighbor to help get him to the hospital.

GERMANY: *Dude, it's cheaper to keep her...* A jealous husband in Germany hired assassins who four times botched hit jobs on his wife. The first attempt failed when the target never showed; the second when a group of school children disrupted the killer; a third came when a neighbor sauntered by; and finally when the woman managed to escape the attack.

GERMANY: *SIEG HEIL? (Hail Victory)* It is unlawful in Germany to manufacture, possess or display any objects glorifying the Third Reich. Recently, German prosecutors have been investigating an artist who created a series of garden gnomes with their arms raised in a Nazi salute. Investigators, however, are not sure if the artist is pro-Hitler or just ridiculing the Third Reich. "It will depend on what the artist and the owners of the gallery have to say for themselves," said a prosecution spokesman.

GERMANY: *Gesundhiet!(To your health)* It was reported in July 2009, that a car thief stole the limo of Germany's health minister while she was on vacation in Spain. Someone broke into the room of Health

Minister Ulla Schmidt's chauffer, grabbed the car keys and made off with the black Mercedes, said a Health Ministry spokesperson.

NORWAY: *Bang!* A hunter while trying to bag a moose fired an errant shot that pierced the wall of a cabin and struck a man sitting on his toilet. The injured man was air lifted to an Oslo area hospital with non-life-threatening wounds, police report. The hunter was aiming at the moose and possibly did not see the cabin more than 100 yards beyond the moose.

SWEDEN: *How ridiculous!* Authorities in Sweden are insisting that a hotel install smoke detectors, even though it is made completely of ice. The Icehotel in the small Arctic town of Jukkasjaervi is a hotel that is rebuilt from huge blocks of ice each winter. Now authorities say the hotel must conform to regular building codes by installing smoke detectors before they can be allowed to have an occupancy permit. *RIDICULOUS!!*

ILLINOIS: *She sounds like one of those mad dog prosecutors!* Molly Alexis, an Assistant State's Attorney in Cook County was drunk when she strolled into a lingerie shop called Taboo Tabou in Chicago. When she was asked to leave, Alexis, 33, became belligerent and bit a worker on the leg. We learn further that she has been placed on administrative leave from her job. We wonder why she bit the worker on the leg – why not the hand or the shoulder? *Mad dog prosecutors are defined as the type of prosecutors who wish to prosecute everyone for everything. Biting a store employee on the leg raises the definition to a whole new level.*

FLORIDA: *We now have the legalized use of "chin-prints"* in Florida. Elena Victoria of the wealthy town of Boca Raton leaped out of her car after drunkenly crashing. She was coming from a summer cocktail party. She claimed she had not been behind the wheel. Police, however, found what looked like her chin print in the soft foam of her steering wheel. They then saw a wound on her chin and decided to arrest her for DWI. *Caught by the prints on her little chiny chin, chin...*

ILLINOIS: *Sounds mighty painful... that greeter needed a big bust in the mouth.* A Chicago lady is suing a popular downtown restaurant after its 300-pound, former football player door greeter gave her such a bear hug that one of her breast implants broke. What a mess it all made at the door. She is now suing for damages of $50,000, for pain, suffering and popping. Just the pain and embarrassment alone, in spite of the silicone mess is worth at least a $50,000 settlement.

ILLINOIS: *Who flung poo?* Penelope Pope of Naperville, a small town outside of Chicago, was so fed up with stepping over dog droppings of her neighbors' dog on her sidewalk she took matters into her own hands. We mean she really took matters into her own hands! One evening after work Pope picked up some of the dog droppings (we hope she wore gloves) and flung it at the suspect neighbors' front door. As one might imagine, it made quite a stink. Police charged Ms. Pope with disorderly conduct. She received no jail time, but she hopes the neighbors got the idea to clean up after their pets.

CALIFORNIA: Los Angeles has finally finished preparing for the 1984 Olympic Games! The city announced that it has synchronized all its traffic lights so motorists can more easily navigate clogged streets and vehicle exhaust pollution can be reduced. The job was supposed to be done to handle increased traffic resulting from the Summer Games 29 years ago, but the project fell through the cracks. *OBVIOUSLY!*

OREGON: *Did she get to see his "long form?"* A resident claims in a lawsuit that a female IRS auditor strong-armed him into a sexual relationship by suggesting it was the only way he could get out of tax trouble. After beginning an audit, the woman allegedly showed up at his home and threatened him with tax penalties if he didn't put out.

OREGON: *RING, RING, RING...* A woman is facing a year in prison and a $6,000 fine because her toddler daughter kept accidentally dialing emergency services while playing with mommy's cell phone. Savannah Peyton said she was in the bathroom when her 1-year-old accidentally summoned police. "It was an honest mistake," she said. Police tend to disagree because the kid dialed 911 16 times over a two month period.

OREGON: *Here's another one about cell phones.* Police in Molalla said a woman's phone accidentally butt-dialed 911 and dispatchers suddenly found themselves listening in on a drug chat. Police tracked the phone's GPS signal and arrested two people on drug charges. *So dumb, so dumb...*

CALIFORNIA: *Then, it couldn't have been "doggy style sex!* A janitor in San Mateo was recently convicted of faking an ankle injury to collect workers' compensation payments. What did the evidence show? She was seen running in a park in high heels to her boyfriend. Then, doctors testified she performed a sex act that would have been impossible with an injured ankle.

WASHINGTON: *Wasn't this in a scene from that old movie "Smokey and the Bandit?"* A state trooper chasing two men on motorcycles flipped over his patrol car on I-5 near Tukwila. Instead of racing away, the men stopped their cycles, pointed at the upside down trooper and laughed. They then took off.

WASHINGTON: *Absolutely shocking!* A woman in Washington whose husband was leaving her got back at him by allegedly rewiring his power tools to deliver a powerful electric shock when he used them. She was arrested after he was knocked to the ground while using a 220-volt table saw.

CALIFORNIA: *We believe he misses his Mary Jane.* A marijuana farmer in Southern California has filed a lawsuit against his landlord because his marijuana crop was stolen from his residence. Ryan Avery is demanding $35,000. He might want to be careful with this suit, though. Police say that he is not a legal marijuana grower.

WASHINGTON: *Girls – that's the way the cookie crumbles sometimes.* We learn that when girl scouts from Troop 52853 in Bellevue deposited cookie money at the bank they learned some of their "dough" was no good. Some customer had passed a counterfeit $20 bill to them and the troop will have to absorb the loss.

WASHINGTON: *What we really want to know is how short will those new socks be?* It has been reported that the corrections department estimates it will save $120,000 a year by eliminating juice dispensers and giving inmates juice boxes instead. Also, the department claims it will save another $22,000 by issuing inmates shorter socks.

NEW MEXICO: *We guess he could not toe the line.* A 27-year-old man, who was once accused of biting off a piece of his girlfriend's toe, was arrested again, recently – this time for trying to slice off her big toe with a cigar cutter said Santa Fe police.

TEXAS: *We wonder what kind of surcharge he had been required to pay?* A man broke into the Department of Public Safety's office in Austin, smashed equipment and smeared the word "surcharge" on a lobby wall in feces. He was barefoot and wearing a DMV polo shirt during the rampage. The man, who was charged with criminal mischief, also did $9,000 in damage to police cars in the parking lot.

TEXAS: *Bad advertising for those who wish to arm teachers.* We have learned pro-gun advocates wanting to arm school teachers might want to reconsider. Why? A Texas educator in his first weapons class managed to accidentally shoot himself in the leg. School administrators said the weapon – and not the teacher – malfunctioned.

NEW MEXICO: *Oh Poo...* Albuquerque police are trying to "flush" out brazen bathroom bandits who enter city restrooms and steal auto-flush sensor mechanisms. The thieves pose as plumbers, zero in on Flush-O-Matics and sell them for $30 each on the black market.

NEW MEXICO: *Bet this hurt!* A drunken driver who led N.M. police on a wild chase was stopped after he toppled out of his moving car and was run over by it. The painful end to the chase took place when the man got his vehicle stuck in a ditch, gunned it in reverse and fell out of the door. His legs were run over, but he suffered only minor injuries.

TEXAS: *Talk about getting your panties in a "bunch.* Yes, there is some suspicion that this guy has a weird panty fetish. A kinky thief walked into a Victoria's Secret in Dallas and made off with 130 pairs of panties valued at $1,067. Detectives are probing what styles of lustful lace the man fancied.

BRAZIL: *Ay, Mamacita!!!!!!* A woman has been charged with attempted murder for putting a toxic chemical on her private parts in an effort to poison her husband during love-making. The man wound up in the hospital after the noxious roll in the hay, but he survived. The woman was caught when a test turned up the foul substance.

BRAZIL: *Sounds like no Bzzzzzzzzzzzzz…..*A man held up a sex shop in Brasilia, walking out with a $4,000 gold plated vibrator. The clerk, noting the bandit forgot the charger, said, "I really don't know what he'll do with it. We'll leave it to his imagination."

THE END

ABOUT THE AUTHOR

Professor Birdsong received his J.D. from the Harvard Law School and his B.A. from Howard University. He teaches law in Orlando, Florida.

After graduation from law school, he worked four years at the law firm of Baker Hostetler. He then entered into a varied and distinguished career in government service. He served as a diplomat with the U.S. State Department with various postings in Nigeria, Germany and the Bahamas.

Professor Birdsong later served as a federal prosecutor. After leaving government service, and before he began teaching, Professor Birdsong was in private law practice in Washington, D.C.

www.BirdsongsLaw.com
lbirdsong@barry.edu

ORDERING INFORMATION

New books coming soon!

Dear Reader,

If you liked this book, I would greatly appreciate you writing me a review on Amazon or any other book site.

I look forward to sharing more funny stories with you in future books.

Thank you, I really appreciate your help.

Regards,

Professor Birdsong

Winghurst Publications
1969 S. Alafaya Trail / Suite 303
Orlando, FL 32828-8732
www.BirdsongsLaw.com
lbirdsong@barry.edu

OTHER BOOKS BY PROFESSOR BIRDSONG:

* Professor Birdsong's 77 Dumbest Criminal Stories (Kindle & Paperback)

* Professor Birdsong's 147 Dumbest Criminal Stories: Florida (Kindle & Paperback)

* Professor Birdsong's 177 Dumbest Criminal Stories – International (Kindle & Paperback)

* Professor Birdsong's 157 Dumbest Criminal Stories (Kindle & Paperback)

* Professor Birdsong's – BEST! 207 Dumbest & Weird Criminal Stories (Kindle & Paperback)

* Professor Birdsong's Weird Criminal Law Stories (Kindle)

* Professor Birdsong's "365" Weird Criminal Law Stories for Every Day of the Year (Kindle)

* Professor Birdsong's Weird Criminal Law Stories, Volume 2: Stories From Around the States and Abroad (Kindle)

* Professor Birdsong's Weird Criminal Law Stories, Volume 3: Stories from New York City and the East Coast. (Kindle)

* Professor Birdsong's Weird Criminal Law Stories - Volume 4: Stories from the Midwest (Kindle)

* Professor Birdsong's Weird Criminal Law Stories, Volume 5: Stories from Way Out West (Kindle)

* Professor Birdsong's Weird Criminal Law Stories - Volume 6: Women in Trouble (Kindle & Paperback)

* Professor Birdsong's Weird Criminal Law - Volume 6: Women in Trouble! (Paperback)

* Immigration: Obama must act now! (Kindle)

Leonard Birdsong